Playma

In

The Faith

Vol. 4

Persevere & Finish

<u>DEDICATION</u>

Heavenly Father, have mercy on us. Give us the strength to persevere and finish strong. Help us to keep our focus only on You! In Jesus' name, Amen!

CONTENTS

SCRIPTURE

23 And someone asked Him, Lord, **will only <u>a few</u> be saved** *(rescued, delivered from the penalties of the last judgment, and made partakers of the salvation by Christ)? And He said to them,*

24 **<u>Strive to enter</u> by the narrow door** *[force yourselves through it],* **for many,** *I tell you,* **will try to enter and will <u>not be able</u>.**

Luke 13:23-24 AMPC

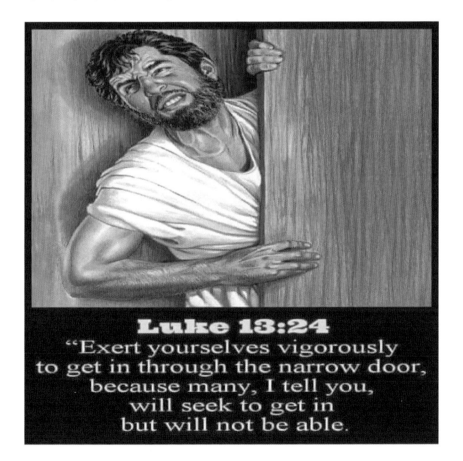

Luke 13:24
"Exert yourselves vigorously to get in through the narrow door, because many, I tell you, will seek to get in but will not be able.

CHAPTER 1

THE NARROW ROAD

Praise the Lord! Through a pure heart, prayer, and meditation of the Word, the narrow road will be made clear to us. If we have a **pure heart** to the Word of God, our eyes will be open, and we will begin to travel the narrow road to Heaven. (*Matthew 5:8*)

> ⇒**11** And He replied to them, To you it has been given <u>to know the secrets *and* mysteries</u> of the kingdom of heaven, but to them it has not been given. **12** <u>For whoever has [spiritual knowledge], to him will more be given *and* he will be furnished richly so that he will have abundance;</u> but from him who has not, even what he has will

be taken away.¹³ This is the reason that I speak to them in parables: **because having the power of seeing**, they do not see; and *having the power of hearing, they do not hear, nor do they grasp and understand.*

⇒¹⁵ For this nation's heart has grown gross (fat and dull), and their ears heavy *and* difficult of hearing, **and their eyes <u>they have tightly closed</u>, lest <u>they see</u> *and* perceive with their eyes, and hear *and* comprehend the sense with their ears, and grasp *and* understand with their heart**, and turn *and* I should heal them.

¹⁶ *But blessed* (happy, fortunate, and to be envied) *are your eyes because they do see, and your ears because they do hear*. **Matthew 13:11-13,15-16 AMPC**

We will understand the secrets of the Kingdom of Heaven if we open our hearts and eyes. If we desire to truly seek after the Lord, the Lord will reveal to us more about the Kingdom through the Holy Spirit. Many people will hear the Word of God and will not understand it. The fault is not on God, it is on them. They may not truly desire in their heart to understand.

⇒**¹³ Enter through the narrow gate**; for wide is the gate and **spacious** *and* **broad is the way** that **leads away to destruction**, and **many** are those who are **entering through it**.
¹⁴ But **the gate is narrow** (contracted by pressure) and **the way is straitened** *and* **compressed that leads away to life**, and **few** are those who **find it**.
Matthew 7:13-14 AMPC

¹³ "***Enter by the narrow gate***. For **the gate is wide and the way is *EASY* that leads to destruction**, and those who enter by it are **many**.
¹⁴ For the **gate is narrow and the way is *HARD*** that **leads to life**, and **those who find it are *few***.
Matthew 7:13-14 ESV

We can look up this same Scripture in many different versions of the Bible and it will be similar. The narrow road is ***HARD!*** This is the only road to Heaven. Only few find the narrow road to eternal life. The road to death (Hell) is wide and ***EASY***.

Jesus is letting us know that the road to Heaven is very difficult. Not many travel the narrow road. Because only few travel it, it can seem lonely.

Remember, we are never alone because we have the Holy Spirit who comforts us and guides us so we can make it Home to the Celestial (Heavenly) City. We also need to stay around Christians who truly obey the commands of Jesus. <u>Please find a church that teaches **ALL** of the commands of Jesus</u>. **This is how you will know that the <u>truth</u> is in that church**. (*1 John 2:3-5*)

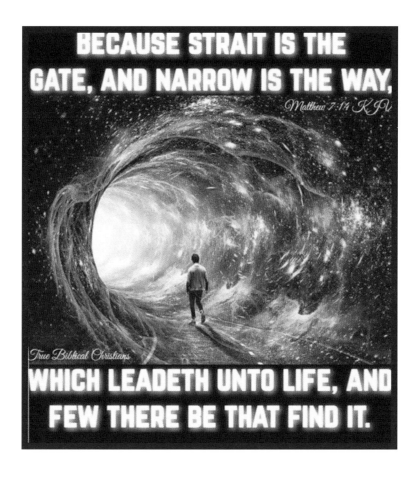

Where Is Your Heart?

⇒**¹⁹ Lay not up for yourselves treasures upon earth**, where moth and rust doth corrupt, and where thieves break through and steal:

²⁰ <u>But lay up for yourselves treasures in heaven</u>, where neither moth nor rust doth corrupt, and where thieves do not break through nor steal:

²¹ For where your treasure is, <u>there will your heart be also</u>.

Matthew 6:19-21 KJV

In this world, we will be tempted to live for earthly treasures. The world tells us to get "**the bag (money).**" Our Lord commands us to not store up earthly treasures. He also commands us to not serve money.

If we are building earthly treasures, then our heart is in the world. If we are building Heavenly treasures, then our heart is with the Lord. It cannot be both. Jesus tells us that we cannot do both. If we try to build earthly treasure and Heavenly treasures, we will only love one and hate the other. It's impossible to serve two masters.

24 No one can serve two masters; for either **he will hate the one and love the other**, or he will stand by *and* be devoted to the one and despise and be against the other. **You cannot serve God and mammon** (deceitful riches, money, possessions, or whatever is trusted in).
Matthew 6:24 AMPC

•**If Jesus is our master, His commands will be priority in our life.**

•**If money is our master, we will serve sports, jobs, school, and other activities before the Word.**

 <u>**Example #1**</u>: Your job wants you to support or be silent about same sex marriages.

⇒If you serve money, you will support or keep silent about it.

⇒If you serve Jesus, you will speak the truth and will be willing to lose your job for the sake of the Gospel.

<u>**Example #2**</u>: Your supervisor is asking you to do something that is wrong and goes against the

Bible. If you do not perform this duty you will lose your job.

⇒If you serve money, you will say, "It's just business, I have to feed my family." You end up doing the duty and denying Jesus' command.

⇒If you serve Jesus, you will not do the duty and lose your job.

If Jesus means more to us than anything else, our actions have to back up our words.

⇒We cannot be **cowards** when its time to make difficult decisions for our faith. It takes *courage* to stand up for the truth!

My wife and I walked away from our jobs at a church because they wanted me to stop preaching on certain topics in the Bible. I was the youth pastor and they did not fully believe in obeying **ALL** of the commands of Jesus (one topic was not swearing oaths - *Matthew 5:33-37* / James 5:12). We both worked there part-time making $36K a year. When I was told to cease and desist from those topics, my wife and I resigned the very next day.

What would we both say to Jesus on Judgement Day if we stayed because we needed the money? We did not have a savings and we were living check to check. However, the Lord has provided for us and has taken care of all of our needs. Money cannot help us on Judgement Day.

> • **We have decided to stay faithful to the Lord and His teachings!**

Heart Is Truly For The Lord

We can truly see a person's heart in their actions. I see many pastors and preachers today who drive luxury cars or buy expensive clothing. I do full time ministry and I believe that we should live in modesty and not in opulence. My first reason is that there are too many people in the world who are homeless and hungry.

⇒**Many people can be offended, if I as a minister of the Gospel, drive a luxury vehicle and there are high school kids who barely eat every day?** I could sell the car and purchase a modest used vehicle and use the rest of the money to feed people and buy cars to give to single moms or dads in need.

It hurts my heart to hear about preachers who have a helicopter to fly them from one side of town to another in the same city. What is wrong with driving? That money spent on a helicopter can be used to help many people who are hurting.

There are some teenagers committing suicide because they can't handle the hardships. Many of them do not know Jesus.

⇒**It's wrong to lead other Christians to believe that godliness is obtaining wealth and riches. <u>That is a false Gospel</u>.**

³ But **<u>if anyone teaches otherwise </u>and does not assent to the sound *and* wholesome messages of our Lord Jesus Christ** (the Messiah)

and the **teaching which is in agreement with godliness** (piety toward God),

[4] **He is puffed up with pride** *and* stupefied with conceit, [although he is] woefully ignorant. He has a morbid fondness for controversy and disputes *and* strife about words, which result in (produce) envy *and* jealousy,
quarrels *and* dissension,
abuse *and* insults *and* slander, and base suspicions,

[5] And protracted wrangling *and* wearing discussion *and* perpetual friction among **men who are corrupted in mind and bereft of the truth, who imagine that godliness or righteousness is a source of profit** [a moneymaking business, a means of livelihood]. *From such withdraw*.
1 Timothy 6:3-5 AMPC

[17] Now I beseech you, brethren, **mark them** which **cause divisions and offences contrary to the doctrine which ye have learned; and** avoid them.

18 For they that are such **serve not our Lord Jesus** Christ, <u>but their own belly; and by good words and fair speeches deceive the hearts of the simple</u>.
Romans 16:17-18 KJV

CHAPTER 2

PERSECUTION OF THE CHRISTIAN

Praise the Lord for His mercy and grace! I am so thankful for the Holy Spirit who gives us strength during trials, tribulations, and persecution.

10 **Blessed are they which are persecuted for righteousness' sake**: for theirs is the kingdom of heaven.

11 **Blessed** are ye, **when men shall revile you**, and **persecute you**, and <u>**shall say all manner of evil against you falsely, for my sake**</u>.

12 **Rejoice**, and <u>be exceeding glad</u>: for great is your reward in heaven: for so persecuted they the prophets which were before you.

Matthew 5:10-12 KJV

⇒The Greek word for **blessed** is *Makarios*: *blessed, happy, fortunate, well off.*

•The Greek word for **persecuted** is *diōkō*:

1.*to pursue (in a hostile manner)*

A.*in any way to harass, trouble, molest one, to persecute.*

B.*to be mistreated, suffer persecution on account of something, to run after, follow after: someone.*

Jesus says that we are blessed when we are persecuted or suffer for our faith. <u>**People will say things about us that are not true**</u>. They will falsely accuse us. Jesus tells us to <u>rejoice</u> and be <u>glad</u> when it happens because we will have a GREAT reward waiting for us in Heaven.

20 **Remember** the word that I said unto you, **The servant**
　　<u>**is not greater than his lord. If they have persecuted me,**</u>
　　<u>**they will also persecute you**</u>; if they have kept my **<u>saying, they will keep yours also.</u>**

²¹ But all these things will <u>they do unto you for my name's</u>
<u>sake, because they know not him that sent me.</u>
John 15:20-21 KJV

⁴ **Jesus** answered them, ***Be careful that no one***
misleads you [deceiving you and leading you into
error].

⁵ For **many will come in** (on the strength of) **My**
name [appropriating the name which belongs to
Me], saying, I am the Christ (the Messiah), and ***they***
will lead many astray.

⁶ And you will hear of wars and rumors of wars; see
that you are not frightened *or* troubled, for this must
take place, but the end is not yet.

⁷ For nation will rise against nation, and kingdom
against kingdom, and there will be famines and
earthquakes in place after place;

⁸ All this is but the beginning [the early pains] of
the birth pangs [of the intolerable anguish].

⁹ Then **they will hand you over to suffer**
affliction *and* **tribulation and <u>put you to death</u>**,
and you will be hated by all nations for My name's
sake.

10 And then **many will be offended** *and* **repelled** *and* **will begin to distrust** *and* **desert [Him Whom they ought to trust and obey]** *and* **will stumble and fall away and betray one another** *and* **pursue one another with hatred.**

11 And **many** false prophets will rise up and deceive *and* lead many into error.

12 And the ***love of the great body of people will grow cold*** because of the multiplied lawlessness *and* iniquity,

13 But he who endures to the end will be saved.
Matthew 24:4-13 AMPC

⇒Jesus **WARNS** us to **NOT** be led into *ERROR*.

⇒There will be **MANY** false prophets and false teachers of the Word.

⇒Jesus tells us that we will be put to death.

⇒During this time **MANY** believers will fall away from the faith.

⇒**Only those who <u>endure</u> to the <u>END</u> will be <u>SAVED</u>!**

¹² Beloved, **think it not strange concerning the fiery trial which is to try you, as though some strange thing happened unto you:**
¹³ **But rejoice**, inasmuch as **ye are partakers of Christ's sufferings; that, when his glory shall be revealed, ye may be glad also with exceeding joy.**
¹⁴ **If ye be reproached for the name of Christ, happy are ye; for the spirit of glory and of God resteth upon you**: on
their part he is evil spoken of, but on your part he is glorified.
1 Peter 4:12-14 KJV

⇒**¹⁶** Yet **if any man suffer as a <u>Christian</u>, let him <u>not be ashamed</u>**; but <u>let him glorify God on this behalf</u>.
1 Peter 4:16 KJV

So, since Christ suffered in the flesh *for us, for you*, **arm yourselves with the same**
thought *and* **purpose** [patiently to suffer rather

than fail to please God]. **For whoever has suffered in the flesh** [having the mind of Christ] is <u>**done with [intentional] sin**</u> *[has stopped pleasing himself and the world, **and pleases God**],*

2 So that he can no longer spend the rest of his natural life living by [his] human appetites *and* desires, *but [he lives] for what God wills*.
1 Peter 4:1-2 AMPC

⇒22 Confirming the souls of the disciples, and ***exhorting them to continue in the faith***, and that <u>***we must through much tribulation enter into the kingdom of God***</u>.
Acts 14:22 KJV

•The Greek word for **tribulation** is *thlipsis*: *oppression, affliction, pressure, distress.*

12 Yea, and <u>**all** that will live godly in Christ Jesus</u> **shall suffer persecution.**
2 Timothy 3:12 KJV

⇒The Apostle Paul says that **ALL** who live godly in Christ Jesus will suffer persecution. Everyone who follows Jesus' commands will go through tough times.

In 2010, I was playing professional football with a team in the UFL. I was very open about my faith and talked about Jesus in the locker room and during practice. ***A coach who claimed to be a Christian, reprimanded me after a football game for saying, "Glory to God, coach."*** We had just won a game and the coach was upset and said to me, "Not now!" I was so confused because why would any Christian get upset at another Christian for giving glory to God? I was released from the team a week after the incident.

⇒ **Persecution will come from people who claim to believe in Jesus.**

In 2012, I worked for a grocery store as a part time clerk. One of the employees asked me a question during lunch, about how I felt about same sex relationships. I told her the truth and gave her Scripture from a pocket Bible that I kept with me to read on my breaks. She later reported me to the store manager, and I had a meeting with the manager. I told the manager that she asked me how I felt, and I told her the truth. I was not afraid of losing my job or of being written up. I will gladly speak about Jesus freely and will gladly suffer the consequences that come with it.

⇒**I refuse to be a coward!**

ACTS 14:22B
...THROUGH MANY TRIBULATIONS WE MUST ENTER THE KINGDOM OF GOD.

CHAPTER 3

THE LAWLESS BELIEVER

Thank You, Lord, for Your Word which is holy and true! Thank You for revealing to us that holiness is obeying Your commands. Help us, Lord, to follow Your teachings so we may have eternal life! (*Revelation 14:12*)

21 Not everyone who says to Me, Lord, Lord, will enter the kingdom of heaven, but <u>he who does the will</u> of My Father Who is in heaven.

22 <u>Many</u> will say to Me on that day, **Lord, Lord**, have we not prophesied in Your name and driven out demons in Your name and **_done many mighty works in Your name?_**

23 And then **I will say to them openly** (publicly), I never knew you; **depart from Me**, **you who act wickedly [disregarding My commands].**
Matthew 7:21-23 AMPC

Lord, have mercy! I studied this Scripture because I did not want the Lord to tell me, "Depart from Me." I needed to understand why Jesus tells these believers to depart from Him. It has now become very clear! Do you remember in **_Volume 1_**, the **Key Scripture**?

19 Go ye therefore, and **teach all nations**, baptizing them in the name of the Father, and of the Son, and of the Holy Ghost:

20 **Teaching them to observe ALL things whatsoever I have commanded you**: and, lo, I am with you always, even unto the end of the world. Amen.
Matthew 28:19-20 KJV

⇒**How many pastors, preachers, teachers, and ministers do you know or have heard teach ALL of the commands of Jesus?**

In Matthew 7:23, the word **iniquity** or **wickedness** in the Greek is *anomia- the condition without law (because ignorant of it, or violating it), contempt and violation of law.*

If a Head Coach wants me to teach 100 plays, but I only teach 40-70 plays, am I being obedient? **No!** If I only teach 80 plays, then I am not on the same page with the Head Coach. How can the football players obey all 100 plays if they do not know them?

⇒**How can Christians obey ALL of the commands of Jesus, if ALL are not being taught?**

• **If Pastors, preachers, and ministers of the Word are Holy Spirit led,**

wouldn't the Holy Spirit lead them to be obedient and teach ALL that Jesus commands?

- **There is nothing wrong with learning other things in the Bible, but it is important to <u>TEACH what Jesus said to TEACH first!</u>**

- **It <u>needs</u> to be taught, so people can KNOW their Lord's commands.**

Why All Commands Are Not Taught

One of the reasons why ALL of the commands of Jesus are not taught is because of **FEAR!**

When a church has over 50% of its congregants who are divorced and remarried, a pastor may be afraid to teach or tell them that the relationship they are in, is adultery (*Mark 10:1-12*).

Those congregants who may give a lot of money to the church will probably get offended and leave.

Erasmus who was a catholic priest, Dutch philosopher, and Christian humanist, called Jesus' and Paul's teachings about marriage, divorce, and remarriage to be "***Monstrous!***" He also stated that, "We need to reinterpret Scripture and not depend on the past."[1] Many other reformers introduced heresy into the church. This is one reason why the divorce rate is very high.

I sometimes have a hard time preaching on that topic because there are so many people who are living in adultery. I even have people who support my ministry living in adultery. Once I was aware of their situation, I told them the truth according to the Word in love. They know my heart and they know that I didn't make it up. It is in the Bible and Jesus commands it. **If they leave, then they leave**. Hopefully, they will repent.

---

[1] Erasmus of Christendom by Roland Bainter, NY; Charles Scribner's Sons. 1969 pp.229-231

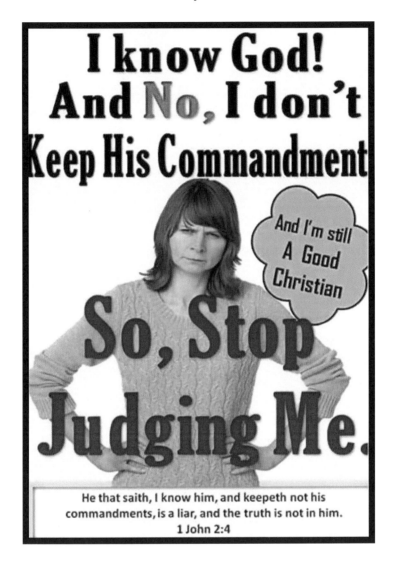

⇒John the Baptist was beheaded because he told Herod, the Ruler of Galilee, that his marriage was unlawful and in adultery. (*Matthew 14:1-12*)

Whenever I have fearful thoughts of preaching

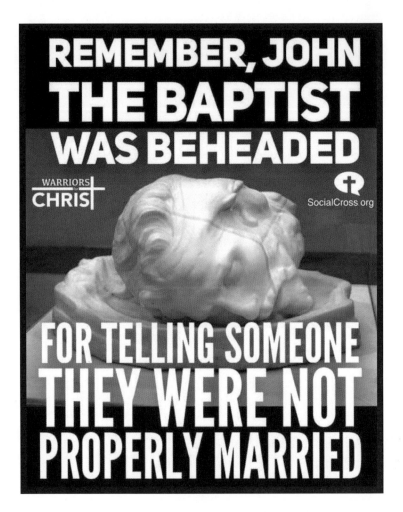

on tough topics, my <u>fear of God outweighs my fear of man</u>. ***Whoever hears the Word but does not*** *repent (make a change)* **will <u>not</u> enter into the Kingdom of Heaven**.

Another reason why ALL of the commands are not taught is because some pastors, preachers, and ministers <u>do not know</u> that they are supposed to be preaching ALL of the commands.

⇒If your church doesn't teach **ALL** of the commands of Jesus, you can ask them to see if they are aware of what **JESUS commanded** them **to TEACH!**

⇒If they do know, but have not taught them, then please *respectfully* and *lovingly* correct them to teach what our **LORD** commands. They will be held accountable on Judgement Day for not teaching what our Lord commanded them to teach.

The truth of God is in churches that teach ALL of the commands of Jesus.

3 And **hereby we do know that we know him, <u>if we keep his commandments</u>.**

4 He that saith, I know him, and <u>keepeth not his commandments, is a liar, and the truth is not in him</u>.

5 But **whoso keepeth his word, in him verily is the love of God perfected**: <u>hereby know we that we are in him</u>.
1 John 2:3-5 KJV

Example Of Disregarding Jesus' Commands

There have been recent shootings in churches. Churches now have security and Christians who carry guns in the church. It concerns me because Jesus commanded us to not resist the evil person.

38 Ye have heard that it hath been said, An eye for an eye, and a tooth for a tooth:

39 But I say unto you, That ye <u>resist not evil</u>: but <u>whosoever</u> shall smite thee on thy right cheek, turn to him the other also.
Matthew 5:38-39 KJV

43 Ye have heard that it hath been said, Thou shalt love thy neighbour, and hate thine enemy.

⁴⁴ But I say unto you, <u>Love your enemies</u>, <u>bless them</u> that curse you, <u>do good to them</u> that hate you, and <u>pray for them</u> which despitefully use you, and persecute you;
Matthew 5:43-44 KJV

⇒Jesus commands us to not resist or defend against evil. To resist someone is to defend. Jesus is talking about self-defense.

⇒The Greek word for **resist** is *anthistēmi- to set one's self against, to withstand, oppose.*

⇒Jesus also commands that we **love** our enemies, **bless** them, **do good** to them, and **pray for** them.

Where did the church get the idea that it is okay to bring guns or weapons into church to protect the congregants?

³⁵ And he said unto them, **When I sent you without purse, and scrip, and shoes, lacked ye any thing**? And they said, **Nothing.**
³⁶ Then said he unto them, But now, he that hath a purse, let him take it, and likewise his scrip: **and <u>he</u>**

that hath no sword, let him sell his garment, and buy one.

37 For I say unto you, that this that is written must yet be accomplished in me, And he was reckoned among the transgressors: for the things concerning me have an end.

38 And they said, **Lord, behold, here are two swords. And he said unto them, It is enough.** Luke 22:36-38 KJV

Jesus sent them out with nothing before. Jesus was about to be arrested, and He told them to grab items that they would need. If Jesus told them to grab a sword to defend themselves, then He would be contradicting His own command. So, I looked up the Greek word for sword.

⇒**Sword** in the Greek is **machaira**- *a large knife, used for killing animals and cutting up flesh; a small sword, as distinguished from a large sword: curved sword for a cutting stroke / a straight sword, for thrusting.* Strongs G3162 Thayer's Greek Lexicon from Blueletterbible.org

⇒In the English language, we have words that have multiple meanings. This sword was also used for killing animals and cutting up flesh for food. (*Acts 10:12-13*)

⇒**Jesus <u>rebuked</u> Peter for using the sword in self-defense!**

52 Then **said Jesus unto him, Put up again thy sword into his place: for all they that take the sword shall perish with the sword.**

53 <u>Thinkest thou that I cannot now pray to my Father</u>, and he shall presently give me more than twelve legions of angels?
Matthew 26:52-53 KJV

- **Jesus says all who take or draw the sword will die by the sword.**

- **We can obviously see that Jesus did not mean for them to use it to protect themselves.**

12 For **we <u>wrestle not against flesh and blood</u>**, but against principalities, against powers, against the rulers of the darkness of this world, against spiritual wickedness in high places.
Ephesians 6:12 KJV .

3 For though we walk in the flesh, **we do not war after the flesh**:

4 (**For the weapons of our warfare are not carnal**, but mighty through God to the pulling down of strong holds;)
2 Corinthians 10:3-4 KJV

⇒**Paul is saying we do NOT fight against flesh and blood, which is people.**

⇒**We do NOT war or fight with earthly weapons (guns, knives)!**

There is **NO** Scripture in the New Testament, that talks about the church defending themselves against attacks. We can read the Didache of the Apostles, Early church history, and Polycarp and they all support what Jesus commands. *Turn the other cheek.*

I recently, questioned a pastor who believed that we should have guns in church for our defense against attackers.

I asked him, "Would you pick up a gun and shoot the attacker if Jesus was there kneeling in prayer?"

He responded by saying, "If Jesus was standing there, I wouldn't have to shoot the attacker (smiling emoji)."

I said to him, ***"The comfort that you would have if Jesus was there should be the same because we have the Holy Spirit. Why would you act different with the Holy Spirit?"***

Jesus said, "**16** And I will pray the Father, and **he shall give you another Comforter**, <u>that he may abide with you for ever;</u>"
John 14:16 KJV

Why Believers Can't Obey Some Commands

The reason why people can't obey some

commands is because they are <u>breaking the first and greatest commandment.</u>

37 Jesus said unto him, **Thou shalt love the Lord thy God with <u>all</u> thy heart**, and with <u>all</u> thy soul, and with <u>all</u> thy mind.

38 This is the **first** and **great** commandment. **Matthew 22:36-37 KJV**

If we love God with ALL / 100% of our heart, we will desire to obey 100% of His commands.

⇒The rich young ruler could not follow Jesus because he did not love God with ALL of his heart. He loved God with some of his heart because he obeyed some of the commands. He lacked the first and greatest commandment. (*Matthew 19:16-27*)

Many believers in America have a hard time with turning the other cheek. If you obey it, many will call you a coward for not defending your family.

⇒I see why they cannot obey what Jesus says. They love their own life and family more than they love Jesus and His commands.

[37] He that <u>loveth father or mother more than me is not worthy of me</u>: and he that <u>loveth son or daughter more than me is not worthy of me</u>.
Matthew 10:37 KJV

[25] He that **loveth his life shall lose it**; and <u>he that hateth his life in this world shall keep it unto life eternal</u>.
John 12:25 KJV

[24] For **<u>whosoever will save his life shall lose it</u>**: but whosoever will lose his life for my sake, the same shall save it.
Luke 9:24 KJV

⇒I love Jesus and His commands more than my own life and family. I put His commands above all!

There are many Christians overseas who are tortured, beaten, raped, and killed. They <u>do not</u>

defend themselves or resist their attackers. Are they cowards?

The courageous Christians are the ones who are willing to suffer and die. The cowards fight back to defend themselves out of fear. In the early church, many men, women, and children died in the coliseum. The apostles died horrible deaths. Peter was crucified upside down. He saw his wife die before him. His last words to her was, "Remember the Lord." That's real faith!

This is one reason why I pray for and support ministries like *Open Doors* and *Voice of the Martyrs*. The stories of the boldness of these Christians is very inspiring.

What can we do if attackers come in the church? We can pray for them or escape. Jesus did command that we can flee from our attackers.

23 But **when they persecute you in this city, flee ye into another**: for verily I say unto you, Ye shall not have gone over the cities of Israel, till the Son of man be come.
Matthew 10:23 KJV

I used to fight every day my junior year in college. I am physically fit and could easily fight back. What is holding me back? What is leading me to be obedient to my Lord's command? My love for Jesus.

"15 If ye love me, keep my commandments."
John 14:15 KJV

Yes it would be very difficult if my family was attacked. What helps me to endure is the Holy Spirit and knowing its only temporary. My family and I will be in the Celestial City with

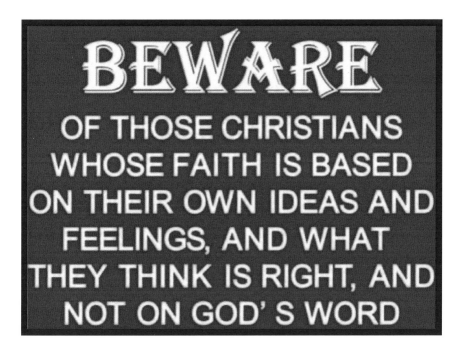

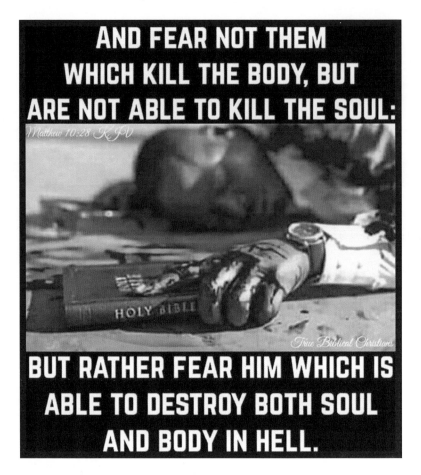

AND FEAR NOT THEM WHICH KILL THE BODY, BUT ARE NOT ABLE TO KILL THE SOUL: *Matthew 10:28 KJV* BUT RATHER FEAR HIM WHICH IS ABLE TO DESTROY BOTH SOUL AND BODY IN HELL.

Jesus, where there is no more pain and suffering. Death is good for us because we follow Jesus! (*Philippians 1:21*)

Beware **of those who make *void* the Commands of Jesus!**

There are many who teach the heretical doctrine of Christian self-defense and encourage

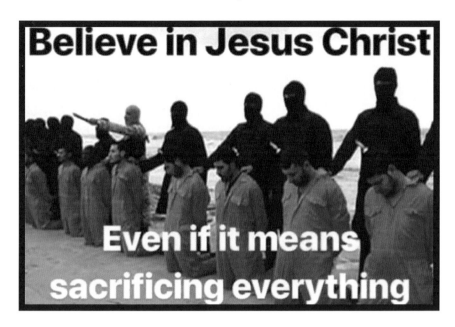

Christians to purchase guns to shoot their attackers. They do not realize that they are teaching Christians to break multiple commands of our Lord Jesus.

<u>**Commands that are broken:**</u>

1. **Do not resist the evil person, turn the other cheek. Recompense to no man, evil for evil. Vengeance belongs to the Lord. Avenge not ourselves (*Matthew 5:39 / Romans 12:17-21*). How is shooting our attacker leaving vengeance to the Lord?**

2. **Love them, bless them, do good to them, and**

pray for your enemies (*Matthew 5:43-48*). How is shooting our attacker loving them, blessing them, doing good to them, and praying for them?

3. **Do unto others as you would have them do unto you. (*Luke 6:31*)**

4. **Fear <u>not</u> those who kill the body, but fear Him who after kills has the power to cast soul and body in Hell (*Luke 12:4-5*). People fear for their lives and they defend out of fear.**

5. **Be merciful as God is merciful (*Luke 6:36*) How is shooting our attacker being merciful to them?**

6. **We shall not murder (*Matthew 19:18*). Is it Holy Spirit led to shoot an attacker and take their life?**

7. **Forgive those who sin against us (*Matthew 6:14-15 / Acts 7:60*). How is shooting our attacker showing an act of forgiveness towards them?**

Taking the attacker's life, who is living in

wickedness, will perish. Taking their life cannot be Holy Spirit led because it is not God's will for the wicked man to perish, but to give him time to repent. (*2 Peter 3:9*)

Jesus explains what these believers are doing who teach away His commands.

9 And He said to them, **You have a fine way of rejecting [thus thwarting and nullifying and doing away with] the commandment of God in order to keep your tradition** (your own human regulations)!

10 For Moses said, **Honor** (revere with tenderness of feeling and deference) **your father and your mother,** and, He who curses or reviles or speaks evil of or abuses or treats improperly his father or mother, let him surely die.

11 **But [as for you] you say, A man is exempt if he tells [his] father or [his] mother, What you would otherwise have gained from me [everything I have that would have been of use to you] is Corban, that is, is a gift [already given as an offering to God],**

12 **Then you no longer are permitting him to do anything for [his] father or mother [but are letting him off from helping them].**

13 **Thus <u>you are nullifying and making void</u> and of no effect [the authority of] the Word of God through your tradition, which you [in turn] hand on. _And many things of this kind you are doing_.**
Mark 7:9-13 AMPC

CHAPTER 4

THE CELESTIAL CITY

Praise the Lord! The only goal in life is to make it to the Celestial City. In the End, this is **ALL** that matters. Is your name written in the Book Of Life? Did you enter through the Gates Of Heaven? Jesus tells us to strive to enter through the narrow Gate. Many will try to enter into the City and will not be able to enter.

> ⇒**24 Strive to enter in at the strait gate**: <u>for many</u>, I say unto you, <u>will seek to enter in</u>, and **shall <u>not</u> be able**.
> **Luke 13:24 KJV**

Getting in the Gates has to mean everything to us. It has to be our **only goal** in life. If we make this our only goal in life, we will live a life that is pleasing to the Lord.

It is important that we get sin out of our lives. We cannot live in sin and expect to make it into the Gates. Look at what Jesus says about getting rid of sin in our lives.

43 And **if thy hand offend thee, cut it off**: <u>it is better for thee to enter into life maimed</u>, **than having two hands to go into hell**, into the fire that **never shall be quenched**:

44 Where their worm dieth not, and the **fire is not quenched**.
Mark 9:43-44 KJV

- **Lord, have mercy! A fire that never goes out.**

⇒If any social media platforms are causing you to sin, delete the apps.

⇒If you have friends who are doing things against the commands of Jesus, <u>do not</u> hang out with them.

⇒**Do whatever you must do <u>to not sin</u> against God!**

26 For **<u>if we sin wilfully after that we have received the knowledge of the truth</u>**, there remaineth no more sacrifice for sins,

27 But a certain fearful looking for of judgment and fiery indignation, which shall devour the adversaries.

28 He that despised Moses' law died without mercy under two or three witnesses:

29 Of how much sorer punishment, suppose ye, shall he be thought worthy, who hath **trodden under foot the Son of God, and hath counted the blood of the covenant, wherewith he was sanctified, an unholy thing**, and hath done despite **unto the Spirit of grace**?

30 For we know him that hath said, Vengeance belongeth unto me, I will recompense, saith the Lord. And again, The Lord shall judge his people.

31 It is a <u>fearful thing</u> to fall into the hands of the living God.
Hebrews 10:26-31 KJV

- **If you know the right thing to do and you do not do it, it is sin.** (*James 4:17*)

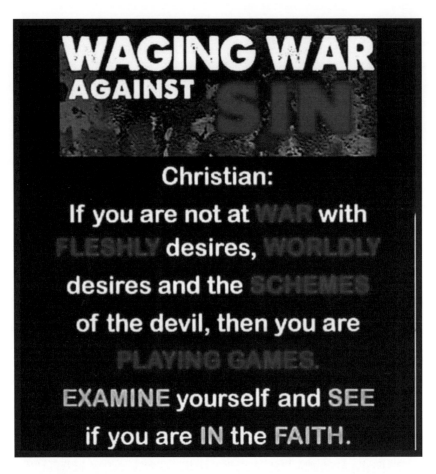

WAGING WAR AGAINST SIN

Christian:
If you are not at WAR with FLESHLY desires, WORLDLY desires and the SCHEMES of the devil, then you are PLAYING GAMES.

EXAMINE yourself and SEE if you are IN the FAITH.

21 **Keep yourselves** in the love of God, looking for the mercy of our Lord Jesus Christ unto eternal life.

22 And of some have compassion, making a difference:

²³ And others <u>save with fear</u>, pulling them out of the fire; hating even the garment spotted by the flesh.

²⁴ Now <u>unto him that is able to keep you from falling</u>, and to present you faultless before the presence of his glory with exceeding joy,
Jude 1:21-24 KJV

⇒**We must keep ourselves in the love of God and the Lord will keep us from falling.** (*John 15:9-10*)

¹² Wherefore, my beloved, **as ye have always obeyed**, not as in my presence only, but now much more in my absence, **<u>work out your own salvation with fear and trembling</u>**.
Philippians 2:12 KJV

⇒**Yes, we need to workout our own salvation with <u>fear</u> and <u>trembling</u>. We need to be very afraid of sinning against God.**

¹² **<u>Take heed</u>**, brethren, lest there be in any of you an evil
heart of unbelief, in departing from the living God.
¹³ **But exhort one another daily**, while it is called
To day;

lest any of you be hardened through the deceitfulness of sin.
Hebrews 3:12-13 KJV

Look at the language the apostles are using. They are warning the believers. This is not going to be easy. The narrow road is very hard. The devil hates us and will try to keep us from getting to the Celestial City.

And I saw a new heaven and a new earth: for the <u>first heaven and the first earth were passed away</u>; and there was no more sea.

2 And I John saw the holy city, new Jerusalem, coming down from God out of heaven, prepared as a bride adorned for her husband.

3 And I heard a great voice out of heaven saying, Behold, the tabernacle of God is with men, and he will dwell with them, and they shall be his people, and **God himself shall be with them, and be their God**.

4 And God shall wipe away all tears from their eyes; and there shall be no more death, neither sorrow, nor crying, neither shall there be any more pain: for the former things are passed

away.
Revelations 21:1-4 KJV

⇒ **18** And the building of the wall of it was of jasper: and **the city was pure gold, like unto clear glass.**
Revelation 21:18 KJV

And he shewed me **a pure river of water of life, clear as crystal, proceeding out of the throne of God and of the Lamb**.

2 In the midst of the street of it, and on either side of the river, was there **the tree of life**, which bare twelve manner of fruits, and yielded her fruit every month: and the leaves of the tree were for the healing of the nations.

3 **And there shall be no more curse**: but the throne of God and of the Lamb shall be in it; and his servants shall serve him:

4 And they shall see his face; and his name shall be in their foreheads.

5 And there shall be no night there; and they need no candle, neither light of the sun; for the Lord God giveth them light: **and they shall reign for ever**

and ever.
Revelation 22:1-5 KJV

⇒**No more pain, No more suffering, and No more tears.**

⇒**Joy, peace, love, and happiness forever.**

⇒**Whatever it takes, whatever I need to sacrifice, I will do!**

[14] **Blessed are they that do his commandments**, that they may have right to the tree of life, and **may enter in through the gates into the city**.
Revelation 22:14 KJV

If you do not make it into the Celestial City, you will be cast out into Hell. Your family and friends <u>will not</u> remember that you ever existed.

⇒Christians in Heaven cannot remember those who <u>did not</u> make it because it would cause them pain and suffering knowing their loved one did not make it.

⇒The Lord will have to erase their memory of you.

⇒You <u>do not</u> want your name to be forgotten forever.

YOU MUST MAKE IT INTO THE CELESTIAL CITY! <u>YOU HAVE TO MAKE IT!</u>

I LOVE YOU BROTHERS AND SISTERS IN CHRIST!

Printed in Great Britain
by Amazon